Upside Down, Turn Me Around

Daniel in the Dangerous Den

Written by Bek and Barb
Illustrated by Bob Ostrom

Faith Kidz® is an imprint of
Cook Communications Ministries, Colorado Springs, CO 80918
Cook Communications, Paris, Ontario
Kingsway Communications, Eastbourne, England

DANIEL IN THE DANGEROUS DEN
© 2006 by Cook Communications Ministries for text and illustrations

All rights reserved. No part of this book may be reproduced without written permission, except for brief quotations in books and critical reviews. For information, write Cook Communications Ministries, 4050 Lee Vance View, Colorado Springs, CO 80918.

First Printing, 2006
Printed in India
1 2 3 4 5 6 7 8 9 10 Printing/Year 10 09 08 07 06

Cover: Sandy Flewelling
Interior Design: Sandy Flewelling and Julie Brangers

All Scripture quotations, unless otherwise noted, are taken from the Holy Bible: New International Version®. NIV®. Copyright © 1973, 1978, 1984 by International Bible Society. Used by permission of Zondervan. All rights reserved.

ISBN: 0781443911

Daniel in the Dangerous Den

Daniel and King Darius were good friends. The king trusted Daniel more than anyone else he knew.

"Daniel," he said, "I am making you the top leader over my whole kingdom."

Other leaders were jealous of Daniel. They decided to trick King Darius into making a law that would get Daniel in trouble.

"King Darius," they said, "we have an idea. For thirty days, everyone should pray only to you."

"If anyone breaks this law, he must be thrown to the lions."

Daniel heard about the new law, but he refused to pray to King Darius. Instead, he prayed to God in front of his open window, where everyone could see him.

The leaders were glad they caught Daniel breaking the law and rushed to tell the king. "King Darius, we saw Daniel praying to God instead of you. Now you must throw him to the hungry lions."

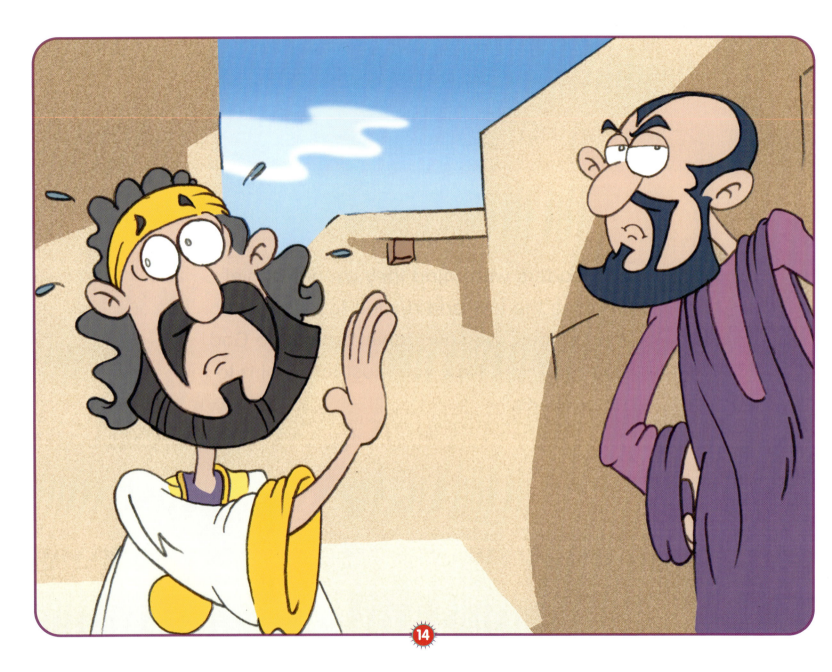

King Darius was upset when he heard this bad news, because he loved Daniel. "There must be some way to save Daniel from the lions," he said.

But as hard as he tried, the king couldn't find a way to save his friend.

He couldn't break his own law.

So the king gave the order, and the men threw Daniel into the lion's den.

"Daniel," cried King Darius, "may your God rescue you." Then the king sadly walked back to his palace.

That night the king was so worried about Daniel, he was sick to his stomach and couldn't eat a thing. He didn't sleep a wink, either. The king hoped his good friend would survive. As soon as it was light, he ran to see if Daniel was still alive.

"**D**aniel!" the king cried out. "Did your God save you from the lions?" The king waited anxiously.

"My king, I'm still here!" Daniel answered. "God sent an angel to shut the mouths of the lions, and they did not hurt me. I don't even have a scratch!"

King Darius was overjoyed. "Pull Daniel out of the pit," he ordered.

Then he gave another command. "From now on, all my people must honor and follow Daniel's living God."

Daniel in the Dangerous Den

Life Issue: I want my child to follow God instead of man.

Spiritual Building Block: Courage

Do the following activities to teach your child to turn to God for courage:

Sight: Look for pictures of people who show courage daily, such as firefighters, police officers, nurses, and disabled people.

Sound: Talk to your child about times when he or she needs to have courage. Pray with your child to ask God for his courage in these situations.

Touch: What does courage look like? Print out 1 Corinthians 16:13 or Deuteronomy 31:6. Cut out the pictures of courageous people you found. Make a collage around the Bible verse.

Upside Down, Turn Me Around

BIBLE STORIES

Moses Parts the Sea

Written by Bek and Barb
Illustrated by Tony Kenyon

The Israelites were in trouble. The Egyptians were coming after them. They could see Pharaoh and his army getting closer and closer. The Israelites were trapped between Pharaoh's army and a sea so big they couldn't get across. They panicked. "What are we going to do?" they cried.

Moses said, "Be still and trust the Lord. God will fight for us. Only God can save us from Pharaoh's army."

The Lord told Moses to stretch his hand out over the water. Moses obeyed; a powerful wind blew the water into high walls that rose up on either side of a dry path.

The trail stretched all the way across to the other side.

The Israelites ran between the walls of water to get away from Pharaoh and his men.

But the Egyptian army followed them right onto the dry ground. What were the Israelites going to do now?

God was their only hope. He told Moses to stretch his hand over the water again. The walls crashed down and swallowed Pharaoh and all of his men.

Every Israelite reached the other side safely. They had seen God's mighty power. He had saved them from the Egyptians. God's people prayed and sang songs with thankful hearts.

Moses Parts the Sea

Life Issue: I want my child to learn that God can do the impossible.

Spiritual Building Block: Faith

Do the following activities to help your child turn to God at all times:

Sight: Visit a lake or get out a map and show your child large bodies of water. Discuss how the Israelites couldn't have escaped from Pharaoh and his army without God's mighty power.

Sound: Talk about the word *trust* with your child. Trust means to put your faith and hope in God. Say to your child, "Tell me about a time when you trusted in God." Tell your child about a time that you had to trust in God. Thank God together for his care and faithfulness.

Touch: Tell you child to stand in front of you with his or her back to you. Hold your arms out and tell you child to fall backward into your arms. Talk about trusting in God even when we can't see him.

Paul and Silas and the Prison Prayer

Life Issue: I want my child to praise God in all situations.

Spiritual Building Block: Praise

Do the following activities to encourage your child to praise God:

Sight: Have your child draw a picture of what it looks like when he or she praises God.

Sound: Ask your child about things he or she can praise God for. Sing a song of praise together.

Touch: Gather objects with your child that will remind him or her of what to praise God for.

That same night the jailer's whole family believed in Jesus.

While it was still night, the jailer brought Paul and Silas to his house; he fed and cared for them.

"No we haven't," Paul said. "We're still here."

The jailer was so happy he fell to his knees. "Your God is amazing," he said. "What must I do to know him the way you do?"

Paul answered, "Believe in the Lord Jesus Christ and you will be saved." The jailer knew Paul was right and believed with all his heart.

The earthquake woke the jailer. When he saw that the prison doors were open, he was afraid because he knew he would be in trouble. "Oh, no!" he said. "What am I going to do? All the prisoners have escaped."

Suddenly there was a powerful earthquake. The ground shook. The prison walls crumbled. The doors sprang open, and all the prisoners were set free.

The prison was cold and dark, but Paul and Silas were not afraid because they knew God was with them. In the middle of the night they prayed and sang songs of praise to God. The other prisoners were surprised.

"Punish them," the judge commanded. "Throw them in jail!"

The soldiers beat Paul and Silas. "Make sure they don't escape," the soldiers said when they handed the men over to the jailer.

The jailer in charge threw Paul and Silas into the prison and locked them in chains.

They grabbed Paul and Silas and dragged them to a judge. "These men are teaching things we don't like," they told the judge.

One day when they were on their way to a prayer meeting, Paul and Silas met a slave girl who needed to be saved. They talked to her about Jesus. Her owners didn't like what Paul and Silas told her. They became angry.

Paul and Silas were God's servants who traveled around, telling people how Jesus could set them free from their troubles. But some people didn't like what Paul and Silas had to say. That is how it was in the town of Philippi.

Upside Down, Turn Me Around

Paul and Silas and the Prison Prayer

Written by Bek and Barb
Illustrated by Alastair Graham